Choosing a Career as a Coach

Coaching is a natural career choice for athletes and other sports enthusiasts.

Choosing a Career as a Coach

Jeanne Nagle

The Rosen Publishing Group, Inc.
New York

For Lar, Keith, and the other coaches who shared their knowledge and experience.

Published in 2001 by The Rosen Publishing Group, Inc.
29 East 21st Street, New York, NY 10010

Copyright © 2001 by The Rosen Publishing Group, Inc.

First Edition

All rights reserved. No part of this book may be reproduced in any form without permission in writing from the publisher, except by a reviewer.

Library of Congress Cataloging-in-Publication Data

Nagle, Jeanne M.
Choosing a career as a coach / by Jeanne Nagle. — 1st ed.
p. cm. — (World of work)
Includes bibliographical references (p.) and index.
ISBN: 978-1-4358-8667-4
1. Coaching (Athletics)—Vocational guidance. I. Title. II. World of work (New York, N.Y.)
GV711 .N343 2001
796'.07'7—dc21

2001000590

Manufactured in the United States of America

Contents

	Introduction	6
1	Types of Coaches	11
2	Where Can I Coach?	19
3	Related Careers	31
4	What to Expect	41
5	Preparing to Become a Coach	46
	Glossary	56
	For More Information	58
	For Further Reading	60
	Index	62

Introduction

Sometimes it seems like Benny's whole world revolves around sports. He's on a team for every season at his high school—basketball in the fall, ice hockey in the winter, and when spring comes around, it's baseball. This summer, he hopes to spend some time at a camp for tennis players.

When he's not actually playing sports, Benny spends lots of time watching games on television or reading about them in magazines and the newspaper. He and his friends like to talk about their favorite teams and athletes, too, and brag about whose team has the best record.

Benny wants to become a professional athlete one day, but he also has another plan for the future. Someday, he would like to become a coach.

He knows that many coaches were athletes themselves at one time, like him.

Coaches dedicate their time to teaching others the sports they love.

Also, Benny figures because he likes sports so much, the career is a natural fit. Because he plays and watches so many sports, he already knows a lot about strategy, competition, and teamwork.

Benny is pretty sure he would like a career as a coach. How about you?

Each person may have a special reason why he or she wants to be a coach. The one thing they all have in common, though, is that they love sports. Games and activities are not just for fun or a hobby for them—they are a way of life.

For some people, becoming a coach is just the next logical step after being a player for many years. Others may like sports but not be very good at them. Either way, coaching is a way for those who love sports to be involved with them as much as possible. More than that, being a coach is an opportunity to share that love of sports. It is a chance to teach what you know about teamwork, winning, and sportsmanship. Being a coach also lets you be around people who think and feel the same way about competition and sports as you do.

To Be a Coach

What does it mean to be a coach? There are several answers to that question. That's because there are so many parts to being a good coach. There are a number of skills that are needed to be successful in this field.

Being a coach means knowing a lot about a sport, including any rules or techniques needed to help the team improve. More than that, though, these professionals need to be willing and able to share that information with others. Coaches are teachers who use their experience and knowledge to help each individual member of the team become a better player.

This means that coaches must also enjoy interacting with others. They have to work not only with athletes but with other coaches, people associated with the teams or organizations that hire them, and the public that watches their games. Someone who is very shy or likes to be alone more than in a crowd would most likely not enjoy or excel at being a coach.

Someone looking to make it in this field also needs to be a good leader. Coaches need to be good bosses without being too bossy. This means being able to make decisions quickly and accurately, and

Motivating and teaching others to become better players are important in coaching.

then giving directions in such a way that people will not question you but do as you say. It also means being able to take the blame when things go wrong, as well as taking the credit when everything goes right.

Coaches need to be creative, thinking up new plays and ways to win within the boundaries of any given sport. Sometimes they have to do this right on the spot, changing a game plan in the middle of the event to make up for a player being hurt or the other team catching on to the preplanned strategy. Being able to make a complete, cooperative whole out of many individual athletes also takes a good deal of resourcefulness.

Funny as it may sound, coaches need to be excellent cheerleaders, too. They need to find ways to motivate their players to give it their all. The best coaches are upbeat and inspirational. They don't

Choosing a Career as a Coach

just tell their athletes about sportsmanship and good behavior but show these traits through their own behavior.

Finally, coaches also should know how to use their authority wisely and responsibly. It is important that they not push people around, have favorites, hold grudges, or convince someone to do something they know is wrong. Coaches should never use their power as a threat but simply as a tool to get people to reach their best performance.

Basically, coaches need to be smart about sports, both how to play them and how to recognize the changes that are taking place on the field, court, or rink. They need to be creative, take risks, and set a good example for their players. A good coach is a good leader, one who is fair and makes decisions based on what's good for the team, not himself or herself.

> There are many traits and skills that are necessary to be a good coach. Here are some questions to ask yourself.
>
> 1. Do you consider yourself a leader or a follower?
>
> 2. Are you able to balance winning with sportsmanship and teamwork?

1

Types of Coaches

So let's say you've decided you love sports and you have many, if not all, of the traits a good coach needs. Even if you are set on pursuing a career as a coach, you will have a few more decisions to make, including what kind of a coach you would like to be.

Head Coach

The head coach of any team is the big boss. Except for certain star players, the head coach is the most visible member of any team. These are the people that athletes, fans, coworkers, and employers look to as the source for everything that goes right and wrong during the season.

Head coaches make up game plans, work with athletes on skills, and set the overall tone for how practices will be run and how games will be played. More than that, these individuals are in charge of a lot of administrative duties, too. For instance, many coaches have to schedule when they can use a court or field for practice. They also may negotiate renting or buying equipment. Connected with that is the team or department's budget, which the head coach must keep on track. Head coaches also file reports on players and any staff members who work under them. Head coaches who work for colleges or the pros usually take part in scouting and choosing players as well.

Even though they are the bosses, head coaches have plenty of people to answer to. In grammar, middle, and high school work, the head coach is overseen by the school's principal and the school district's superintendent. Colleges and universities have deans and athletic directors who watch over and guide head coaches. Even the pros have people who are higher up than the head coach, namely general managers and team owners.

Assistant Coach

An assistant coach's job duties are explained in his or her job title—he or she assists the head coach. However, this position can mean different things in different situations.

An assistant coach in college or high school could be responsible for a lot of the "grunt work," such as cleaning up and putting away equipment. But they also get to carry out more fulfilling duties, like helping players with skills and figuring out a plan of attack. In college sports and the pros, assistants are very involved in planning and execution during both games and practices.

Assistant coaches for Little League or intramural sports generally get more hands-on

In some cases, assistant coaches work more closely with players than head coaches do.

opportunities to work with players, leaving more of the administrative duties and tasks such as talking with parents to the head coach. Assistants at this level also may be asked to act as referees at games. When this happens, the assistant will have to be impartial, which means he or she must not make any calls that help his or her team unfairly.

Another duty of an assistant coach is to take over when the head coach cannot do his or her job. That is why an assistant needs to know all about running a team, even those duties he or she doesn't generally handle. Perhaps the most important job of an assistant coach is to watch, listen, and learn from the head coach. Many head coaches worked their way up the ladder by being assistants first and by seeing what works and what doesn't.

Specialty Coach

A coach whose work is concentrated in one area is called a specialty coach. For example, in football, there are usually coaches who focus on and deal with problems related to offense, defense, or special teams—the squad of players called in for kick returns and field goals only.

There is extra value in being a specialty coach. Specializing makes you stand out and is one of the factors that helps coaches break into the pros. Specializing also helps because it increases your chances of getting a job with a professional team. After all, there is only one head coach per team, but, depending on the sport, there are usually several specialty coaches for each squad.

Volunteer Coach

If you want to make coaching a career, you are, of course, going to want to get paid for your work. However, you might want to at least consider starting out as a volunteer coach.

One of the biggest factors that will decide whether or not you get a paid coaching job is experience. People prefer to hire someone who not only says he or she can do the job but can prove it with experience. That's where volunteer coaching comes in. By volunteering, you get valuable firsthand and hands-on knowledge about sports and how to lead a team.

Community and recreation sports programs are always on the lookout for people who want to work as coaches. Very few places will turn down an offer to help coach a team for free. Keep in mind, though, that when you volunteer, you will have to show some smarts about the sport you want to coach, such as its rules and regulations. Some programs, such as town recreation departments, may require that their volunteers have CPR and first-aid training. A background check may also be needed, particularly if you plan to work with small children. Check with the organization running the program for the requirements you will have to meet to volunteer.

Randy, Volunteer Coach

I volunteer as an assistant coach for my little brother's basketball team in our

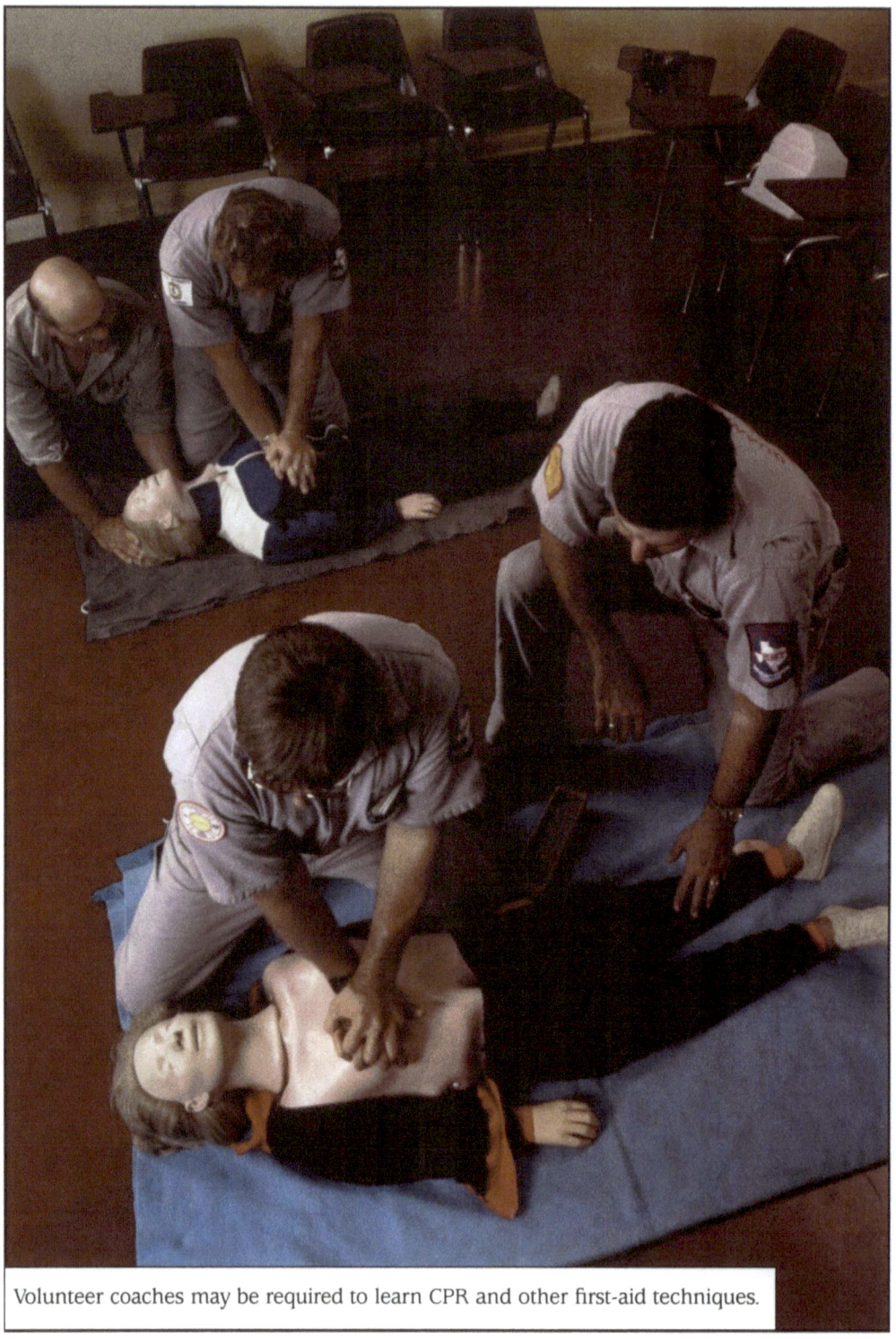
Volunteer coaches may be required to learn CPR and other first-aid techniques.

area's recreation league. They're a group of fifth- and sixth-graders. I run them through drills, and the head coach counts on me to work with individual players on stuff like free throws while he concentrates on the big picture—the whole team.

Believe it or not, I like spending time with the kids. They look up to me because I used to play on my high school team. I enjoy teaching them the stuff I know about the game. It makes me feel like a role model.

But volunteering as a coach is important to me for other reasons, too. I'm hoping to get a part-time job at the rec center, working nights and weekends while I go to the community college. I'm not 100 percent sure if I want to be a coach or a recreation leader. Maybe I'll go to a four-year college and teach physical education. All I really know right now is I want to do something involved with sports and fitness, and working at the rec center will look good on my record.

Before I can get in there, though, I have to get experience. I figure if I volunteer with a program that's connected to the center they'll see what a good job I do and will be more likely to hire me.

I've got it all mapped out. So far, so good. Volunteering was definitely a smart move for my career.

Individual or Group Sports

Another factor future coaches need to consider is whether they want to coach a team or an individual. Usually, the particular sport determines that. For instance, in ice-skating, a coach deals with just one skater at a time. Of course, that coach may work with a couple of different skaters but would do so on an individual basis; he or she would not coach a team of ice-skaters.

> Though they cover many of the same tasks, there are different types of coaches. Here are some questions to ask yourself.
>
> 1. Would you be willing to be an assistant coach or possibly specialize?
>
> 2. Do you want to coach a team or an individual athlete?

Where Can I Coach?

If you are looking to make coaching a career, you will want to be paid for your work. That shouldn't be a problem because there are several types of organizations that offer money to those who coach sports teams.

Schools

The best chance for landing a job comes from schools, where there are sports for each season (baseball, basketball, etc.), and men's and women's teams. Different levels of competition within each sport, like junior varsity or varsity, may each require a separate coach. Whether it's grammar school or junior high school, high school or college, there are several levels of sports teams that need someone to head them up.

The minimum requirements you must meet to get such a job include having a knowledge of the sport or sports you are coaching, either because you have played them yourself or have coached a team at some level. You will also need to know how to work well with kids at different age levels and be certified in first aid and/or CPR. There are probably schools that would also like their coaches to be certified, which means you would have to take special classes and pass a written test that proves you know about coaching and can handle the job.

Some schools like to hire people who have teaching degrees in addition to having experience in sports or coaching. This is because, particularly in grade school on up through high school, many coaches also may teach physical education or health classes. Some even teach subjects that don't have anything to do with sports or fitness. You don't necessarily have to do both, or even be certified as a teacher to get a school coaching job, but it doesn't hurt.

Those who are hired to teach elementary school, junior high, or high school classes as well as coach usually get paid a higher salary for their teaching responsibilities and get a little extra to be a coach. The typical amount earned for coaching, which is called a stipend, is a couple of thousand dollars each year.

There are pressures connected with coaching at any level of school, but as you move up in grade level, things get more intense. When you're coaching a grammar school or junior high school team, most of the stress comes from dealing with parents as well as trying to get the kids to do their best and play by the rules. In high school, things heat up a little bit. There will be players on the team you are coaching who will count on being part of a winning team because

Coaches sometimes teach classes in sports, fitness, health education, or other subjects.

that will help them get scholarships to the colleges they want to attend.

At this level, coaches who are just starting out can expect to earn $20,000 to $23,000 a year. With more experience and years of work under his or her belt, a high school coach can earn up to $40,000 or $50,000 a year.

Colleges and universities are perhaps the toughest school settings in which a person can coach. College sports are one step away from the pros. That means coaching at colleges and universities is just one level beneath coaching a professional team, and so coaches can be under a lot of pressure. They get attention from local and even national media; newspapers, magazines, radio, and television cover the activities of college teams. Sports make a lot of money for colleges so they are treated as very important programs. If a

College and university coaches can be under intense pressure to produce winning teams.

coach does not produce a winning team, he or she could take a cut in pay or, worse, be out looking for another job.

Although there is more pressure involved with coaching a college or university team, the pay is better. Also, those who work at this level usually don't have to teach classes in addition to being a coach. They are free to concentrate only on their teams.

How much money a college coach makes depends on a number of things. One is the division his or her team plays in: Division I, Division II, or Division III. Coaches whose teams are in Division I, which is the highest division, can make salaries in the hundreds of thousands. Some can make nearly $1 million a year.

College coaches also frequently get incentive or performance bonuses, which are tied into how well they do their jobs. A coach might have in his or her contract that if the team wins a certain number of games, the college will pay him or her extra money on top of a regular yearly wage. In addition, some college coaches get special allowances for things like travel. These bonuses and allowances are in addition to their annual salaries.

Club Sports

Colleges and universities support different sports programs, and most of these schools also have official teams. In addition, however, there are groups or teams that get together and play a sport or game that may not be part of the school's usual program. These are called club sports because a group of people join together to play them like they would join another kind of club at school. The team is usually made up of students who have an interest in the sport and enjoy playing it, but view the sport more as a hobby. Rather than taking on a large commitment and perfecting the skills that you must have if you play for an official team, these students prefer to keep it fun and relaxed. Rugby is a typical club sport.

These teams, which compete against club teams from other colleges and universities, need coaches, too. Often, a student who is a junior or senior acts as the coach, while at other times, a teacher or someone who works outside the school but plays the sport will be in charge. Those who coach club sports do not have to be employees of the college that helps support the team.

Club sports like rugby, while more informal than the official sports teams at a school, also require coaches.

Club sports are supported financially by activity fees paid by students, as well as by any fund-raisers the club decides to hold. Club coaches get paid out of money from fund-raising events or from a pool of cash set aside from the fees collected to support the club program. People who coach club sports are usually paid only a small stipend. It's usually not enough to live on by itself, but it is a paid position.

Samantha, Club Coach

I started karate lessons when I was about nine years old. After years of practice and examinations, I now have my brown belt, and I'm hoping to earn a black belt very soon. Karate is something

Coaching a club sport like karate requires just as much effort and responsibility as coaching an official sport.

Choosing a Career as a Coach

I do because it's good exercise for my mind and body. I never figured I would have a job coaching the sport, though.

It all started when some kids from the university I go to asked my teacher, Sensei Williams, if he would like to be their coach. He was too busy to do it, but he suggested that I give it a try. Because I was so advanced in my studies, he felt I could handle it.

I was a little nervous at first. I mean, the people in the club were pretty much my own age, and here I was telling them what to do and helping them with their skills. It wasn't too long, though, before I realized that you don't have to be older to be a good club coach. You just have to know what you're doing and be able to show other people how to master the moves.

This is not a club like the yearbook staff or something. We practice just like our university's football and basketball teams. Even though karate is more about self-improvement, our club competes in intercollegiate competitions with similar groups from colleges in the area.

I get paid about $500 for the whole year, but I don't coach the team just for the money. Mostly I do it because I love karate and it's fun. Also, it's nice to work with a bunch of people who feel the same way about the sport as I do.

Coaching Professional Sports

If you're looking to hit the big time as a coach, you will want to work toward getting hired by a professional sports team. To get there, you need to be a coach who is willing to work hard and have a winning record.

Professional sports are divided into two main categories: minor league and major league. The minor leagues are like a training ground, where both athletes and coaches can get used to the world of professional sports before heading up to the majors. Major league sports are a big business, and those who want to coach at this level have to be tough, smart, and completely professional.

Each one of these categories is considered to be the pros, but fame and money are the two big differences between minor league and major league—those involved with major league sports get more of both. Professional sports coaches can earn millions, especially if they have winning records.

Each pro team has several coaches: a head coach, some assistant coaches, and specialty coaches. This should mean that there are plenty of jobs for anybody looking to make his or her mark in the pros. However, while there are several coaches for each minor and major league team, there are only so many of those positions to be had. In other words, there are only so many teams in a league in each sport, and once those positions are filled, you're out of luck until somebody leaves.

There are also a lot of people who want these jobs—a whole lot more people than there are actual jobs, in fact. Those who do the hiring for professional teams are looking for experience first and foremost. It is highly unlikely that general managers and owners of professional sports teams will hire someone who hasn't either played as an athlete in the pros or spent many years coaching in a successful college or professional sports program. Be prepared to spend years proving yourself if you want to become a coach in the pros.

Community Coaching

There are plenty of organizations right in your own community that sponsor athletics programs. Little League baseball, YMCA leagues, summer recreation programs, and intramural squads all require coaches.

Most of these community sports teams have the same kind of arrangement as school teams, only they are set up by towns, churches, or civic groups instead of by a school. The head coaches perform the same kinds of duties—teaching skills, motivating players, scheduling practices—but also might recruit parents to help out as assistants and referees, or provide transportation or snacks.

Some places that use community coaches feel these individuals should be certified. This means they would have to attend classes or complete a short coaching program of some sort. Most organizations, however, do not insist on certification. The thing to remember about community coaching

Little League baseball is just one example of the many community-based organizations that hire coaches.

Choosing a Career as a Coach

is that most of these positions do not pay well, if they pay anything at all. Even though they may be volunteers, community coaches still put a lot of time and energy into their work—usually during nights and weekends, when they're not working at their regular jobs.

> Several types of organizations run sports programs that need coaches. Here are some questions to ask yourself.
>
> 1. How far do you want to go in your career as a coach?
>
> 2. Would you rather coach children, teenagers, or adults?

Related Careers

Coaching a team or becoming an assistant coach are only two options in this field. You do not actually have to be a coach to do the same kind of work they do. There are a number of jobs that use the same types of skills.

Personal Trainer

Personal trainers have a lot in common with coaches, only they work with individuals instead of teams. They create exercise and fitness programs that are designed to meet each of their clients' needs and goals. For instance, one person may want to lose weight, while another just wants to build up his or her strength.

Personal trainers make up sets of exercises that target what people want to improve about themselves. A personal trainer also demonstrates the best way to do certain exercises, gives advice on nutrition, and watches as clients go through their workouts to make sure they don't give up or get hurt.

Personal trainers help individuals with their exercise regimens, diet, and safety.

Related Careers

A person who wants to become a personal trainer should know about different sports, how groups of muscles work, and what makes a healthy diet. To help them learn all these things, they may decide to get certified. A certificate is a lot like a diploma. It proves that you did the work that was required and you are qualified to be a personal trainer. It is not necessary to become certified, but those who do can make more money.

Personal trainers can work freelance, which means they work for themselves. They also can be hired by gyms, health clubs, or country clubs to work with the organization's customers. Those who work for a gym or club usually get paid a set salary and then, on top of that, get paid a commission, which is a cut of the fee people pay to be trained.

Miguel, Personal Trainer

I guess you could say I started as a personal trainer about six months ago. That's when this guy at the gym asked me how he could build up his arms so they looked like mine. I told him I did at least ten sets of curls every day, and I showed him how to do them.

Next thing you know, he was asking me for advice all the time, and so were some of his friends. The manager at the gym saw this and asked me if I wanted a part-time job as a personal trainer. I loved the idea.

Choosing a Career as a Coach

What a great job! I work at the gym, so either before or after my shift I can do weight lifting or run around the track. I'm doing something I like to do and something I do really well. Plus, it's pretty cool watching somebody I train get fit and healthy. I feel really good about myself when clients ask for my opinion and they take me seriously.

A short while ago my boss said he could pay me more money if I got my certification. So now I'm learning CPR at the local Red Cross and preparing to take an exam so I can be certified.

I never would have thought of becoming a personal trainer if it hadn't been for that one guy asking me questions. Now I can't imagine not making it my career.

Recreation Worker

The people who put together the games and sports that take place through local parks, summer camps, or recreation centers are called recreation workers. They include the folks who coordinate local sports leagues, such as community basketball, and camp counselors.

Recreation workers can be employed by a town, a civic organization such as the YMCA, or a local parks department. Their job is to organize different sports and games and to make sure that everything goes smoothly. Mainly they are in

Recreation workers, such as camp counselors, organize various sports and games.

charge of getting the space and equipment needed to run these programs, as well as signing people up to join the fun.

Recreation work can be a great job. However, many of these positions are only part-time or, as is the case with camp counselors, may take place only in the summer. Anybody who wants to become a recreation worker should keep this in mind before starting out in this career.

Physical Education Teacher

Those who teach physical education classes in schools have basically the same knowledge and experience as a coach. In fact, because they teach different kinds of sports and exercises, they are a lot like coaches.

Physical education teachers are hired by school districts. Although many of them may be athletes themselves, they are not simply jocks who are looking for a steady paycheck. Physical educators are teachers who need to earn certification in order to work in their field, just like those who teach math or science.

Those who teach physical education earn about as much as teachers in other areas. How much that winds up being depends on what level of schooling is involved—elementary, high school, or college—and how much each school district has in its budget to pay teachers. The average starting salary for these kinds of positions is somewhere between $20,000 and $30,000.

Colleen, Physical Education Teacher

My friends used to tease me when I first told them I wanted to become a physical education teacher. They all figured it was such an easy job; all you have to do is show up, make the kids play dodgeball, and then sit around while they do all the work. Wrong!

First of all, I had to study very hard to teach in this field. I had to go to college, where, besides English and history, I took classes in lots of sports and games. I was graded on what I knew about these activities and how well I could do them myself. Then, after I finished all my classes and got my diploma, I still had to take an exam to prove I was qualified to teach.

My job is at a local middle school. I have to make out lesson plans, which means I have to figure out ahead of time what I'm going to teach and how I'm going to teach it. Because I'm so busy during the day teaching, I usually wait until after dinner or the weekend to write my lesson plans.

Planning is very important for my job. It's not enough just to say, "I'm going to teach floor hockey," give the kids a puck and some sticks, and let them go at it. I make sure they practice individual skills, like passing and protecting the

Coaching often involves demonstrating a variety of different skills for each sport.

puck, before they take all they have learned and play a practice game.

A lot of physical education teachers also teach other subjects if they're qualified, or take on other duties. For example, in addition to planning for and teaching all my classes, I am also the coach of our school's baseball team.

I bet those friends who used to tease me about teaching physical education would be impressed if they knew all the work that I do now.

Athletics Director

Athletics directors are basically the bosses of all the coaches who work for them. They work for schools and run the different sports programs their school's offer.

The main responsibility of an athletics director is to plan. These professionals schedule when sports teams will use courts and fields, as well as when each team can practice. They also have to come up with ideas that will make people want to attend games and participate in sports programs, and they are in charge of making sure the budgets for each of the individual teams are in order.

Athletics directors also supervise the work of coaches and their assistants. They not only have their own paperwork and budgeting to do, but they must make sure that all the coaches under them are doing similar work on their own. Also, they need to motivate coaches to work very hard to produce winning teams.

Being an athletics director, much like being a coach, is not a nine-to-five job. Most work nights and weekends in addition to during the week because that is when most games are played. Some do all their work during the school year, but others spread out their work for a full twelve months.

In return for all this hard work, athletics directors get paid pretty well. Most colleges and universities pay between $30,000 and $80,000 for this type of position. Schools that have the most sports at the highest level of play, which is Division I for colleges, usually pay on the high end of the scale.

To get these kinds of jobs, plenty of athletics directors pay their dues by being coaches first.

Choosing a Career as a Coach

Even though there may be several coaches working for a school—one for each sport, and possibly separate coaches for the men's and women's teams—generally there is only one athletics director for each school. That means there are a very limited number of these positions open, so landing one can be difficult. Only the best prepared are chosen. If you would like to be an athletics director, it would be a good idea to get lots of coaching experience, and the more education you have, the better.

There are many different types of jobs that are similar to being a coach. Here are some questions to ask yourself.

1. Do you want to actually run a team, or would you be happy simply doing the same type of work a coach does?

2. Would you be happier working for an organization, or would you like to freelance and work for yourself?

What to Expect

Choosing a career also means you are willing to accept the type of lifestyle that comes with that kind of job. Coaching is no exception. Like any other line of work, it has both pluses and minuses. First, let's look at the tougher parts of being a coach.

The Drawbacks

For one thing, coaching is a lot of hard work, not just the good stuff that you see a coach doing during a game. There is a lot of stuff that goes on behind the scenes in coaching, like doing all the paperwork, reviewing game tapes and the records of opposing teams, and preparing athletes, both physically and mentally. With all these items to take care of, it's no wonder that coaches frequently put in a lot more than forty hours a week. In fact, experts say that these individuals average fifty hours a week working in their chosen profession.

Coaches work not only during practices and games but long before and afterward, too. Beforehand, they have to prepare by going over their lineups and game plans. After, they usually clean up and wrap up, which means reviewing how things went and making the necessary adjustments.

It's tempting to think that things lighten up for coaches in the off-season of their sport, but this is not necessarily the case. Even during the times when a sport is not played, coaches typically remain very busy. They plan for the next season, check out equipment and order replacements, gear up for tryouts, scout, write reports, participate in off-season camps, and even prepare for banquets or speaking engagements.

In addition, some coaches may head up two or three programs within a school or community, which means they are busy starting up in one sport even as they are in the middle of a season in another. The coaches who also act as teachers in a school system split their time between teaching and coaching as well.

Being this busy can add a lot of pressure and stress, which are two things coaches must learn to deal with on a daily basis. There are many different ways in which a coach can get stressed out. Small amounts of free time, feeling the need to win, and dealing with fans and parents are just some of the factors that bring on the pressure.

Then there is the concern about keeping a job. Coaches need to keep a lot of people happy, including fans, athletes, and the people who hire them. As long as a coach has a winning record, chances are he or she will remain employed. This is partly why coaches work so hard. They have to prove they are good at their jobs all the time in order to keep them. This is especially true in the pros and Division I college sports, which have higher competitive standards than lower-level school or community programs.

The Rewards

Of course, there are many rewards to being a coach, too. For starters, coaches are usually respected members of their communities. People love sports and think highly of those who play games and provide entertainment. This includes the folks who head the teams and guide the athletes, since they are very visible leaders who can represent a whole team. Coaches who go on to college or university jobs and the pros can be admired by people across the country and around the world.

Coaches can be so popular, at any level, that they are asked to participate in celebrity dinners and give speeches. Organizers usually pay extra to have guests participate, so coaches can earn extra money in addition to enjoying a bit of fame. At the pro level, a coach's popularity might even land him or her an endorsement deal, where he or she is asked to promote a certain product or service. Endorsement deals can mean really big cash.

As for financial compensation, it is possible for coaches to earn very good salaries. Starting out, especially as an assistant, the money is not great—$18,000 to $22,000—but beginners in many fields do not make very much at first. The average salary for experienced coaches runs somewhere between $22,000 and $48,000. Those who move on to become leaders of Division I college and pro teams, even as assistant or specialty coaches, can make six figures or more.

Sometimes coaches get the extra benefit of being able to travel. Meets, games, and conferences are occasions that take coaches out of town. A trip can be as simple as visiting another city within the state or as exciting as traveling to foreign countries. While it is true that work takes up a lot of time during these trips, coaches usually can schedule at least a few moments to take in the sights and experience different communities and cultures.

All things considered, coaching is a career that, in addition to being a lot of hard work, can be exciting and full of possibilities.

Antonia, Head Field Hockey Coach

This job keeps me pretty busy. During the season we have practices and games. Practices take about an hour and a half each, and games last two or three hours.

On top of that, I do a lot extra. In addition to calling plays and motivating the players, I take notes during games so I can see what kinds of skills need work. Then I have "homework." After I leave school for the day, I review my notes and try to find drills that will help strengthen our weak points.

I try not to let the job take over my whole life, though. I have a boyfriend, and I like to spend time with him and my other friends. Plus, I have to do stuff that everybody else does, like clean my apartment. The trick is to take the job seriously, but not so seriously that you can't think of anything else. If I start to sacrifice everything for coaching, and if all those things make me stress out, then I try to back away a bit. After all, the more pressure I feel, the more intense I'm going to make it for my athletes, and that's not good for anybody. The trick is to find a balance between coaching well and living your life.

A career as a coach is very hard work, requiring patience and dedication. Here are some questions to ask yourself.

1. Are you willing to put a lot of time into your career?

2. How good are you at handling confrontation and pressure?

Preparing to Become a Coach

Now that you have looked into what a career in coaching requires, you need to think about the best way to get a job in this field. There are four main areas that will impress an employer: knowledge, attitude, experience, and preparation.

Knowledge

Knowledge covers an understanding of the rules and skills of the sport (or sports) you want to coach. There are a couple of ways to get that knowledge. As mentioned earlier, you can play the sport yourself. This will give you the chance to learn how the game is played from the inside, which later, when you are a coach, may help you to be better at communicating ideas to athletes.

Another way to gain knowledge is to study successful coaches. See what they do in different situations, and find a style you think would work well for you. You can observe coaches either by watching games on television or by going to live sporting events. Other ways to do this include

Attending live sporting events is a good way to see coaching firsthand.

reading books about famous coaches or asking local coaches if you can talk to them about their careers.

Obviously, you can also study coaching in a formal school setting. Many colleges and universities have degrees in physical fitness and coaching. To earn these degrees, you will need to take classes, write papers, and actually participate in different sports.

You may also decide to take a certification course. To become certified, you must attend a class that covers the fundamentals of coaching and pass a written exam. Organizations such as the National Youth Sports Coaches Association offer certification programs.

Attitude

Despite what the commercials say, image is not everything. A proper, positive attitude is also

College or university classes in coaching or physical education are also an option.

important if you want to win any job, not just a coaching position.

Attitude is how you act, how you show what you're feeling. If you have a crummy attitude—acting like you don't really care whether someone hires you—people are going to be turned off and turn you down flat. Employers want somebody who is interested in more than just making money. They want a person who is enthusiastic and is determined to do the best job possible.

Interviewing: The First Impression

It is not enough just to say you want the job. You need to show it with the way you dress, look, and act, as well as with your words. When you interview for a coaching position, make sure you wear proper clothing: suit and tie for men, dresses or suits for women. Even though you probably won't be wearing these clothes as a coach, you want to make a good first impression. Overall, when you interview, be clean, neat, watch your posture, and show you are eager and willing to take on the job.

Experience

Maybe the most important factor in landing a coaching job is experience. Reading and learning how to coach is fine, but actually doing it is best. That way you can increase your know-how, and practical skills really impress employers.

As mentioned before, playing a sport yourself is good experience. Volunteer coaching is even better. Community programs, as well as several grade schools, junior highs, and high schools, are usually willing to take on volunteer coaches.

If you do go to college to study coaching, you can also get an internship. As an intern, you can train to be a coach by actually working as one. It is a job, only you get paid with class credits and experience instead of cash, although some internships do pay a little bit.

No matter how you get it, experience is extremely helpful if you want to get a job as a coach.

Preparation

The world of athletics keeps growing. Expansion teams, the rising popularity of sports like soccer and lacrosse, and new events such as Ultimate

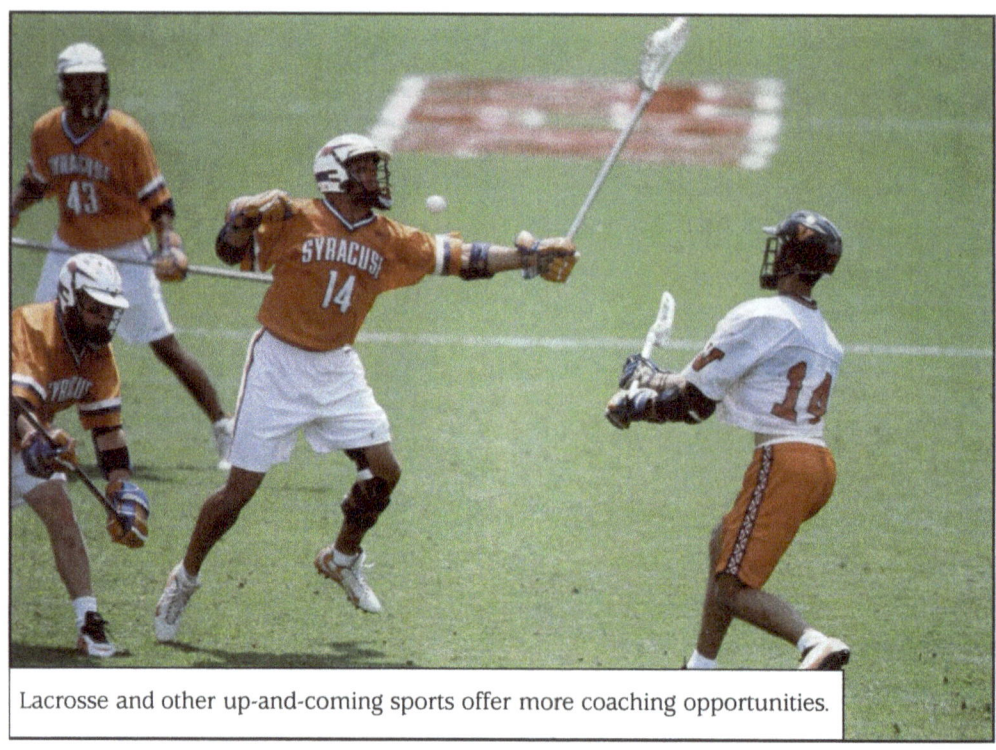
Lacrosse and other up-and-coming sports offer more coaching opportunities.

Frisbee and extreme sports are good news for those who want to coach. There should be a pretty good number of coaching jobs available over the next few years.

Keep in mind, though, that the competition will be tough. Working in sports can be glamorous and exciting, and many people would like to have these positions. You are going to have to do more than apply for an opening if you want to make yourself stand out in the crowd.

Those who want a career in coaching need to go about their job search the same way they would prepare for a game. In other words, they need to do research and plan. The following list includes a few more helpful ideas on how to break into a career in coaching.

Newer sports, including extreme sports like skysurfing, are expanding the athletic world dramatically, and coaches are needed more and more.

Check out lots of ads for coaches in the paper and on the Internet. Put together a list of the skills and experience levels that keep getting mentioned. Then make sure you have the skills most often required.

Network, which means make contacts and get to know people. Get to know the coaches in your school and others who work nearby. Talk to a guidance counselor or someone who is involved in your city's recreation programs. They just might be able to get you started in the field.

Ask a coach you admire to sit down with you for an informational interview. This is not meant to get you work but only to get information about the job. Approach it like it's research for a paper you need to write. Don't take up too much of the coach's time, and try not to seem like you are asking for a job or recommendation.

Read anything and everything you can that is linked to coaching. This includes books, magazines, and newspapers. Absorb sports and coaching like a sponge.

Join a professional coaching organization. Becoming a member increases your chances of meeting useful contacts. Plus, it gives you the inside scoop on being a coach from those who are living the dream now. Check out the resources listed in the back of this book.

Asking advice from a coach can prove invaluable in your own quest to become one.

While your first job in athletics might not be as an actual coach, it is an important step.

Paying Your Dues

Careful planning will help you get work as a coach. All the preparation in the world, however, may not get you a job at the top right away. As you begin your career, you will most likely start out coaching at a small school or recreation program. Other possibilities include taking a part-time or assistant position to begin with, or coaching a sport that is not your favorite.

In fact, the first job you have in sports might not even be as a coach. Accepting a position as a trainer, scout, or administrative staffer for an athletics department is no reason to get upset. The important thing is that you take a job that gets your foot in the door, one that will allow you to prove yourself and eventually become a coach.

A career as a coach may take a lot of hard work and preparation. If you are willing to do whatever it takes, though, you will no doubt find a coaching assignment that is right for you.

> Planning and preparation will help you land a job as a coach. Here are some questions to ask yourself.
>
> 1) Do you think going to college or getting certified will help you achieve your goals?
>
> 2) What contact do you have with coaches already, especially in your own town?

Glossary

athletics director   The person who is in charge of a school's athletics department. An athletics director would be a coach's boss.

certification   Acquired when you take a class in coaching and pass a written test. Certification helps prove you know about coaching and can handle a job in the field; not necessarily a requirement, certification can boost the career of someone who wants to coach.

club sports   Sports played at colleges that are not part of a standard, official team. Such teams can be competitive with other club teams and are usually funded through a school's athletics department or student-run organizations.

Divisions I, II, III   How college-level sports are broken down, based on factors such as number of sports and amount of scholarships/financial aid offered. Division I is the highest division and therefore usually pays its coaches the most.

internship A job performed by a student or other beginner to gain experience in a field. These are generally unpaid positions, although some might offer a small salary.

personal trainer A fitness expert who teaches individuals a skill or technique and then monitors the individuals' performances.

physical educator Someone who teaches physical education at a school. The former term for such a person, "gym teacher," is now considered an insult and should not be used.

special teams A group of players that perform specialized tasks. In football, special teams players are the ones who come on for field goals and punt returns.

specialty coach Coach who concentrates on one area of a game, such as offense or defense.

stipend A fixed salary or allowance paid to someone for doing a job.

For More Information

In the United States

American Alliance for Health, Physical Education, Recreation, and Dance
1900 Association Drive
Reston, VA 20191
(800) 213-7193
(703) 476-3400
Web site: http://www.aahperd.org
e-mail: ginfo@aahperd.org

National Fastpitch Coaches Association (NFCA)
409 Vandiver Drive, Suite 5-202
Columbia, MO 65202
(573) 875-3033
Web site: http://www.nfca.org
e-mail: nfca@nfca.org

National Federation of Professional Trainers
P.O. Box 4579
Lafayette, IN 47903-4579
(800) 729-6378

Web site: http://www.nfpt.com
e-mail: nfpt@nfpt.com

National High School Athletic Coaches Association
P.O. Box 4342
Hamden, CT 06514
(800) 262-2495
(203) 287-0238
Web site: http://www.hscoaches.org
e-mail: office@hscoaches.org

In Canada

Coaches Association of British Columbia (CABC)
#3 6501 Sprott Street
Burnaby, BC V5B 3B8
(604) 298-3137
Web site: http://www.coaches.bc.ca
e-mail: info@coaches.bc.ca

Coaching Association of Canada
141 Laurier Avenue West, Suite 300
Ottawa, ON K1P 5J3
(613) 235-5000
Web site: http://www.coach.ca/cachome.htm
e-mail: coach@coach.ca

For Further Reading

Christina, Robert W., and Daniel Corcos. *Coaches' Guide to Teaching Sports Skills.* Champaign, IL: Human Kinetics Publications, 1988.

J.G. Ferguson Publishing. *Preparing for a Career in Sports (What Can I Do Now).* Chicago: Ferguson Publishing, 1998

Jensen, Clayne R., and Jay Naylor. *Opportunities in Recreation and Leisure Careers.* Lincolnwood, IL: VGM Career Horizons, 2000.

Nagle, Jeanne. *Careers in Coaching.* New York: The Rosen Publishing Group, Inc., 2000.

Packer, Billy, and Ronald Lazenby. *Why We Win: Great American Coaches Offer Their Strategies for Success in Sports and Life.* Lincolnwood, IL: Masters Press, 1999.

Rhodes, Richard, and Steven Haywood. *Basic Coaching Skills: Building Leadership in Youth Sports.* Caldwell, ID: Griffith Publishing, 2000.

For Further Reading

Schnake, Don. *Coaching 101: Guiding the High School Athlete and Building Team Success.* Elk Grove Village, IL: Richview Press, 1996.

Index

A
athletics director, 12, 38–40

B
baseball, 19
basketball, 19, 34

C
camp counselor, 34, 36
club sports, 23–26
coach,
    assistant, 12–14, 18, 27, 28, 31, 39, 43, 44, 54
    community, 28–30, 49
    head, 11–12, 14, 27, 28, 39
    specialty, 14, 18, 27, 44
    volunteer, 15–17, 30, 49
coaching,
    after being an athlete, 7, 19, 28, 46
    becoming certified, 20, 28, 47
    for club sports, 23–26
    for college sports, 12, 19, 21–23, 28, 43, 44
    cons of, 21–22, 41–43
    getting a job, 15, 19, 46–55
    for high school/junior high school, 12, 19–21, 42, 49
    for professional sports, 12, 14, 21, 27–28, 43, 44
    pros of, 43–44
    related careers, 31–40
    salaries earned, 20, 21, 22–23, 24, 27, 30, 43–44
    skills needed for, 8–10, 15, 19–20, 28, 49, 52
    studying in college, 47, 49
    and teaching classes, 20, 22, 36, 42
    types of, 11–18
community/recreation programs, 15, 28–30, 43, 49, 52, 54
CPR, 15, 20

Index

D
dues, paying your, 54

E
equipment, 12, 36, 42

F
first aid, 15, 20
football, 14

G
game plan, 9, 11, 12, 42
general manager, 12, 28

I
ice-skating, 18
internships, 49

J
job interviews, going on, 48–49

L
Little League, 12, 28

M
major league, 27
minor league, 27

N
National Youth Sports Coaches Association, 47
networking, 52

P
parents, 14, 20, 28, 42
personal trainer, 31–34
    becoming certified, 33
physical education teacher, 36–38
    becoming certified, 36

R
recreation worker, 34–36
referee, 14, 28
rugby, 23

S
scouting for players, 12, 42
sports,
    in colleges, 21–22
    as hobby, 7, 23
    knowing rules and techniques, 8, 15, 33, 46
    love of, 7, 8, 11
    practices, 11, 12, 28, 39, 41
sportsmanship, 8, 10
stipends, 20

T
team owner, 12, 28
teamwork, 8, 10

About the Author
Jeanne Nagle is a freelance writer and a senior editor at Hobart and William Smith Colleges in upstate New York, where she makes her home.

Photo Credits
Cover © Brian Spurlock/SportsChrome USA; p. 2 © SW Production/Index Stock Imagery; pp. 7, 32 © Robert Llewellyn/Pictor; p. 9 © Jeffrey Blackman/Index Stock Imagery; pp. 13, 35 © SuperStock; p. 16 © Bob Krist/Corbis; p. 21 © Rob Gage/FPG; p. 22 © Brain Masck/Allsport; p. 24 © Paul A. Souders/Corbis; p. 25 © Chip Henderson/Index Stock Imagery; p. 29 © Mark Gibson/Index Stock; p. 38 © Chris Minerva/Index Stock Imagery; p. 47 © Eric Figge/Index Stock Imagery; p. 48 © Kent Knudson/Pictor; p. 50 © Doug Pensinger/Allsport; p. 51 © Zefa Visual Media/Index Stock Imagery; p. 53 © Patricia Barry Levy/Index Stock Imagery; p. 54 © Donald Graham/Index Stock Imagery.

Design
Geri Giordano